SPENDTHRIFT TIME

SPENDTHRIFT TIME

Poems for Lily

Roger Averill

National Library of Australia Cataloguing-in-Publication Data
A catalogue record for this book is available from the National Library of Australia

Paperback ISBN: 978-0-6487282-4-5
Hardback ISBN: 978-0-6487282-3-8

The river carries me off and I am that river.
I was made of wretched stuff, mysterious time.

—Jorge Luis Borges

For Lily Mallett Averill

CONTENTS

BIG GIRL

I's a big girl,
yes, I am.
I can do everything
a big girl can.

Run, jump, skip & hop,
dance & jive until I drop.
Brush my hair, brush my teeth,
say 'Hi' to Bruno; give him a leaf.

I's a big girl,
yes, I am.
I can do everything
a big girl can.

Walk to Sydney Road & back,
ride my trike without a stack.
Blow my nose when its snotty,
use the toilet, never the potty.

I's a big girl,
yes, I am.
I can do everything
a big girl can.

Play with friends & with Nancy,
choose my clothes, nice & fancy.
Put my runners on my feet,
refuse to use the booster seat.

I's a big girl,
yes, I am.
I can do everything
a big girl can.

Twirl my skirts round in a circle,
ride Mum's bike, watch us hurtle.
Draw and paint pretty pictures,
use a needle, make real stitches.

I's a big girl,
yes, I am.
I can do everything
a big girl can.

There is just one thing I'm yet to do,
I haven't learnt to sleep right through.
Mum & Dad have begged and pleaded,
but turning three is all I needed.

Now I's a big girl,
I *really* am.
I'll sleep right through
'til seven am.

September 2004

SERIOUS

If you know a little girl
Who uses acorns instead of money,
Be sure to say she's serious
And never call her funny.

If you ask her what she wants to eat
And all she says is 'honey',
You're allowed to say she's serious,
But must never suggest she's funny.

And if she says the moonlight
Makes her bedroom look all sunny,
Be careful to call her serious,
And not to say she's funny.

Now if this little girl
Happens to be called Lily,
You might say she's rather solemn,
But, please, don't *ever* call her silly.

September 2005

IS FIVE A BIG NUMBER?

Is five a big number?
Tell me it's true.
It's bigger than one,
But how about two?

Is five a big number?
Please tell me more.
It's bigger than three,
But what about four?

You know I can whistle,
My fingers, they click.
If pricked by a thistle
I stop crying real quick.

Is five a big number?
It must be, I'm sure.
You can't be this clever
And still only be four.

I don't care if you tease,
But you shouldn't be cruel.

Five *is* a big number—I know—
'Cause I'm ready for school.

September 2006

VEGETABLES

They say I don't like vegetables,
Which is true in many ways,
Though I eat them in tuna mornay,
Or disguised in bolognaise.

It's just that when I see them
Lying naked on the plate,
My mouth goes dry and scratchy
And my taste buds get irate.

You see, veggies can't be trusted,
They're never what they seem.
Pretending to be happy things,
They're actually devious & green.

Broccoli looks like a tree,
Tempting me to climb,
But when I go to get a grip
Its trunk all turns to slime.

Carrots can be crunchy,
And I eat them out of habit,
One a month—never more—
For fear of turning rabbit.

Now beans, they look all smiley
When you see them upside down,
But turn the plate the other way
And their smile becomes a frown.

Zucchinis are for meanies,
They remind me of a truncheon;
Something coppers hit you with
As they throw you in the dungeon.

Cauliflowers live a lie;
They must think I come from Mars.
I know they're not a flower,
'cause I can't fit them in a vase!

My family all love potatoes,
Which I think is mighty fine,
And 'cause I'm such a sharing girl
I always give them mine.

I've tried every trick I know
To rid green monsters from my life,
Dropped broccoli on the floor,
Hidden beans beneath my knife.

But now I know they're good for me
I take vegetables by the dose,
Three greens a day, with evening meals
—Chops, sausages or roast.

September 2007

PLAYING SCHOOL

'Shhh! Be quiet, Muffin McClay,
Miss Lily's coming, she's on her way.'
Big Ted rushed back from his post at the door
Then sat with the others on a mat on the floor.

High heels clicking as she entered the room,
Miss Lily swept in like an elegant broom.
'Good morning,' she said, 'girls and boys!'
'Good morning' back, said all the toys.

Red Roo jumped high, still at attention,
Hoping to avoid yet another detention.
Little Dog did her best to sit up tall,
Which was very hard for a dog so small.
'Is that your straightest?' Miss Lily called out.
'Yes, Miss,' said Little Dog, with a quivering snout.

'Right, then, who can tell me what we're doing today?'
'I can, Miss!' blurted Muffin McClay.
'How many times have I told you—it's such a bore—
Put up your hand, or in your case, a paw?'
'I know, Miss, I'm sorry. It won't happen again.
It's just I'm excited about counting to ten.'

Miss Lily went to the whiteboard in order to write,
But her grip on the pen was none too tight.
Her nails, you see, were wonderfully long
But they'd turned her fingers into miniature tongs.
She wrote the numbers one to four,
But then dropped the pen on the wooden floor.

When Monkey swung down and scooped it up,
His tail knocked over the teacher's cup.
Fearing trouble, he quickly took flight,
Climbing the wall, he perched on the light.
'Get down this instant!' screamed Miss Lily.
But while Monkey was a chimp, he wasn't silly.
So he clung to that globe for all he was worth,
Orbiting round like the moon circling Earth.

Miss Lily's face went red with rage,
'If I catch you Monkey, you'll go in a cage.'
She tried to swat him, like killing a fly,
But Monkey and the globe just spun on by.

The other toys laughed at the humorous sight
Of Miss Lily getting giddy from the swirling light.
Tripping into Tiny Ted, then over her chair,
Miss Lily crashed to the floor, her legs in the air.
Feeling dizzy, chucky, really unwell,
She crawled to her table and reached for the bell.

But Monkey grabbed it first, and making it chime,
'This Miss is dismissed,' he announced with a rhyme.
The toys left the room in a raucous stampede,
Trampling their teacher without any heed.

Battered and bruised, poor Miss Lily looked up,
Her head in a puddle from the toppled teacher's cup.
'When I dreamt of teaching,' she said to herself,
Looking at the books all thrown from the shelf.
'When I chose this profession, I never meant this.
Perhaps I could change and become a dentist.'

September 2008

SHOES

I wish I were an insect,
A spider even better.
Imagine, eight legs and feet
Shoed in vinyl, canvas, leather!

My mornings, then, wouldn't be so sad,
Because I wouldn't have to choose
Between boots, sandals, runners, thongs
—I'd simply wear *all* my shoes.

Zips, straps, velcro, laces:
That's how we became attached,
Like a hen is to her chickens
Right after they have hatched.

Tongues, eyelets, even soles;
My shoes sound half alive.
They need my feet inside them, though,
If I want them to survive.

Which is why I have decided
To become a centipede,

So all my shoes can live,
And on my feet be freed.

September 2009

BAKING BREAD

Some poems, I've found, are hard to cook,
Their pages torn from the recipe book.

They rhyme, but never quite on time;
More of a lemon than a lime.

They're the soufflé that simply refuses to rise,
The cake you bake which shrinks in size.

As you know, you must knead your dough,
Then let it rest so it can grow.

So this poem lies flat, here in my head,
In the hope of one day becoming bread.

September 2010

NUMBERS

Numbers, you know,
Are not my go,

But it's beyond my ken
That you're turning ten.

I remember when you were newly born,
The way we'd cuddle to keep you warm.

And when you were ages one, two and three
My arms seemed like the branches of a tree,

And you a bird sleeping in its nest
Huddled against my beating chest.

Then you got older and could read and write
And I'd give you a hug when I said goodnight.

But look at you now, it can't be true,
That little girl has grown to be you,

All strong and tall and full of vigour
And old enough for a double figure.

I don't really care what age you are,
'Cause I'll always be your old Papa

And though it might seem a big presumption,
I'm sure you'll remain my little Scrumption.

September 2011

A SHORT HISTORY

The other day I pondered this curious thought:
Which came first, the trouser or the short?
Did lap-laps grow long, stretching down to the ground,
Or pantaloons shrink and become buttock bound?

French revolutionaries, I know, were called *san-culottes*
For wearing their trousers right down to their boots.
Taking over from dandies in wigs and knee-breeches,
They taught them the lesson that history re-teaches:
There's nothing more apt than an athletic short,
If what you are playing is a good spot of sport,
But if your intention
Is power ascension,
There's nothing much grouser
Than a long-legged trouser.

Length, they tell me, is much like time,
'Relatively speaking', said Einstein.
So shorts of the past seem suddenly long
Compared with today's torn denim thong.

Even so, I can't help but fear
Impending accidents of the rear.

For if shorts, it seems, are worn much higher,
They'll have to be removed with a surgical plier.

But if the scientists are right
that we need lots of light—
That it's vitamin D
that makes us happy—
Then your shortish obsession
Should ward off depression,
And make your dad glad
Of this semi-clad fad.

September 2012

THE PATH

For eleven years we've trod that path,
Cut through the lane, across the grass,
Noticed the elm tree in all its seasons,
Calling it ours for mysterious reasons.

Early on, when Grace was four,
Strapped to my chest, you'd giggle & roar.
Once you could walk, you refused to ride,
Rejecting the stroller as a matter of pride.
Trotting along, matching my pace,
Holding hands, a smiling face,
You never complained or asked to be carried;
Strangely, it seemed, you liked to be harried.

Over the years—a decade in time—
Our trip developed a rhythm, a rhyme.
Crossing the road, then hesitating,
We'd check if Josefine was 'meditating'.
If her blinds were up, then she was awake,
If down, she said, it was for enlightenment's sake!
We said 'Hi' to Gwen, in her dressing gown,
To Scarlet, too, if she was around,
Then on to Bruno with his coat and cap,
A guide, a compass, on our daily map.

'Harry Verdici,' he'd always say,
Making us smile both ends of the day.

In the blink of an eye,
With a saddened sigh,
You and I will no longer hike
Because your trips to school will be by bike.
Riding with Grace, you'll still take the lane,
Our Elm ever changing, yet always the same.
And in my mind, our tree will stand fast,
A guardian protecting you as you pass.

September 2013

RUNNER'S RAP

For some, I know,
running's not the go.
It's something they do
only when they have to,
like to catch a train
or to dodge the rain,
escape a lion's jaw
or the ravages of war.
For me, though, that's just not the case,
as runnin' *is* my chosen pace.
I never feel better
than when I ditch the sweater,
pull on some shorts,
of the baggy sort,
and, pluggin' my ears with tiny speakers,
jog away in a pair of pimped-up sneakers.
It's kinda true,
I'll admit to you,
that the first steps hurt
when I hit the dirt,
and when the tightness in my chest
begs for me to rest
I suspect I'm insane
to enjoy this pain.

Then stretching my stride,
I begin to glide
& the sound of my feet
as they kiss the street
is the song of the bird
that's never been heard
'cause it flies too high
for the ear or the eye.
The arrow of truth
is like a sparrow on your roof,
it mightn't fly right,
but it stays overnight.
So here's the thing,
without any bling:
like a bird in the air
or a fish in the sea,
I'm never more me
than when my feet run free.

September 2014

TELEVISIONARY

Back in the day—
As the young folk say—
When things were all black and white,
Families communed
In one little room
And watched tellie together all night.

How things have changed
With the astonishing range
Of pads, pods and the phone;
Multiplying like rabbits
The change to our habits,
So now we watch shows on our own.

Through cables, fibres, a satellite's beam,
The content arrives in a ceaseless stream:
Offspring, Friends—the whole Modern Family;
Always there, because they can be.
While others demand a little reaction,
These digital folk are the perfect distraction.

Now, as you know,
I'm a Modern Joe,
And not one who thinks
(Making ludicrous links)

That the electronic flicker
Is the work of the wicca.
It's more that I'm sure
Life's here to be lived,
Not seen through the screen
Of a pixelated sieve.

So, rise up, I say,
From your binary bed,
And don't forget
To lift your head.
Because if you do,
You'll enjoy the view,
The sights, the sounds
Of the world all around:
The endless motion
Of the crashing ocean,
A fleeting cloud,
Its silence so loud.

Life and time, in all its rhythms,
Can't be reduced to algorithms.

P.S.
Let me digress—If you liked this poem, you might
also like …

September 2015

DOGGEREL

(*adj.* An epithet applied to burlesque verse of irregular rhythm;
or to mean, trivial, or undignified verse. Transf. Bastard, burlesque.
The Shorter Oxford Dictionary)

I know it's unusual,
Me talking like this,
But some things can't be said
With a poo or a piss.

Believe me, I've tried,
Just look at the carpet;
Weemails, it seems,
Are hard to interpret.

The problem, you see,
Is our self-appointed bard:
He writes about the family,
Yet leaves me in the yard.

Whatever he sees
Through those weird-windowed eyes,
When he puts it on paper
It comes out as lies.

Eleven years of love,
And not even a mention!

What's a dog got to do
To grab his attention?

To write about Lily
And forget about me,
Is like writing about sailing
And not mention the sea.

It's true, when she was little
Lil found me quite frightening.
But now we're inseparable,
Like thunder and lightning.

There's nothing she likes more
Than to sit round and mooch,
Watching her shows
With her favourite old pooch.

I can't reach the great poet
In his tall tower of words;
So high on his own opinion
He communes only with birds.

So if you can breathe
That rarefied air,
Deliver him this message
Through his cloud of curly hair.

I mightn't know much
About art & literature,
But what I do know I know
For certain and sure.

If you don't want your verse
To read like a mongrel,
Follow my lead and put
The dog back into doggerel.

September 2016

FOOTBALLING DYNASTY

Dad played footy in the seventies.
It was a different game back then.
The ball was kicked long to contests
And all the players were men.

Johnny Cassin gathers,
Takes off down the wing,
Blonde hair streaming.
Bounces once, then again,
Gets round Martello,
Sends a tumbling punt
High into the forward line.
Pack forms,
Maxy Crow in the box seat,
Kelvin Moore right behind.
Good luck marking that.
A-VE-RILL!
What a grab!
Is there nothing he can't do?!
Listen to the crowd.
Where'd he come from, Lou?

Dad played footy in the seventies.
He's never talked about it much,

Not like the blokes whose glory days
Become a pathetic kind of crutch.

Averill extracts the ball from the pack,
Handballs to Foulds, who steadies,
Swings onto his right.
He better get a move on;
There can't be much time on the clock.
Moss marks—too far out to score.
Cowboy Neale minds the mark.
Three points down; the Bombers need a goal.
He gives it a roost—everything he's got.
It's going to be close.
Captain Carl's keeping guard in the goal square.
It's drifting left; it's going to be …
AVERILL!—out of the blue.
He's done it again!
He's marked on the boundary line,
Right on the siren.
This is for the Premiership.
How about the pressure!
The impossible angle,
No daylight between the posts.
Head over the ball,
Robbie Muir yelling advice.
The noise tremendous.
A measured approach …

Don't tell me! Don't tell me it's true!
The boy's kicked a goal!
Essendon's broken the drought.
They've lifted him on their shoulders, Lou.

Dad played footy in the seventies
When all the grounds were local.
They didn't have modern amenities,
and the crowds were wild and vocal.

Carn the Dons!
THWUMP!
SLAP! THUD!
CLUNK!
BALL!
C'mon ump.
That's right, ya can't touch The Bilby,
—Protected bloody species!
Any softer, Bluebaggers,
And they'd serve you in a cone.
BALL!
You blind white maggot,
Did you leave your Labrador at home?

Dad played footy in the seventies.
On the MCG of his mind,
Nan's pencil pines, the Punt Road goals,
The bottle brush, a behind.

Captain, coach and commentator,
There wasn't much he couldn't do:
Kick sausage rolls from the patio,
Special comments from the loo.

Now *I* play footy in the twenty-teens
—it's a different game, all right.
I'm in a comp for all-girl teams
—a win for the feminist fight.

Dad still tries to teach me
What he knows about the game.
'Course he learnt it watching tellie,
But the clichés are the same.

When the going gets tough,
Put your head over the ball,
Keep your feet,
Try not to fall.
When the opposition tackles
Don't give 'em an ounce.
And when you break from the shackles
Take a run and a bounce.
Kicking both feet
Is strangely handy
As you baulk and weave
As a seller of candy.

Straight down the guts
Is the quickest way home,
So why go via Burke
Paris, London or Rome?
When it's your turn to go,
You've gotta fly the flag.
Guide the ball to your boot
If you wanna kick a bag.

Knowing Dad's heroics
Were his greatest work of fiction,
With facts and lack of ability
Being of little or no restriction,
I wonder when he watches me
If the tellie's still in his head,
Not Lou and Peter Landy
But Bruce and Bristle there instead.

Lily Averill gathers,
Takes off down the wing,
Blonde hair streaming.
Bounces once, then again …

September 2017

FOR THE RECORD

for 20 years,
slotted side by side
in a milk crate,
musting
in the shed,
they sweated
in their plastic sleeves.
mute.
neglected.

their spinning stilled,
emotions trapped,
fossilised songs
lay buried in the
mounds & furrows
of a vinyl earth.
each disc a planet,
each track tracing
the orbit of another time.
all awaiting the cleaving blade
of that diamond plough.

then,
sceptical of today's

digital (meta)physics,
the immanent god of wifi
—google, play me
it's alright ma
(i'm only bleedin')—
following the trend
toward the tangible,
you dusted off these
relics from your parents'
past.

reading round
the cover,
studying its art,
you reaped what the singer
sowed in some smokey studio
forty or more years ago.
the same sounds
i heard when i
was as young
as you are now.
the same emotions:
yearning,
love, anger,
joy,
hurt, hope.
the sounds of

music's mystery—
saying all the things
that can never be said,
singing the silence
of the never-dead.

September 2018

SPENDTHRIFT TIME

Every year
in winter
when the days
themselves seem
reluctant to wake
and the air nicks
the nostril on its
way to the lung,
I find it hard to believe
that soon
the sun,
which I now seek
through the dining room
window, will
burnish that same pane
with unremitting heat
and fight its descent
in the western sky
like a child
resisting sleep.

How much harder,
then,

to recall
how it was when
you were small?
Yet, like the buds
that appear
at the time
of your birth
each year,
as if to remind us
of summers past
and to warn
of even hotter blasts,
your impish look
or warm embrace
hurtles me back
to when you were indeed
a member of that
smaller race.

How can eighteen years
have slipped so easily by
and you have grown
to womanhood
before my eye?
Time,
the only currency
to truly rise in value

with lessening supply,
has left me poorer
but for the banked memories
of your fierce affections
that I withdraw,
then readily spend,
knowing they replenish,
and with greater interest grow,
comforting me,
I'm sure,
to my very end.

September 2019

LOCKDOWNER

As if with the perforated
Squares of toilet paper
Rationed to us by our
Panic, we wipe away
The days of disease
From our lives,
Tearing time carefully,
Unstitching its seam,
Wasting nothing but
The waste itself,
Learning to live in
The blank repetition
Of recycled swatches
Slowly unspooling,
Day after night after day,
Each one different
In the exact same way.

September 2020

FEARSOME (CRITIQUE)

How dare you write a poem
About a pandemic and call
It a gift! I'm not looking
To cause trouble, an inter-
Generational rift, and, no,
I'm not after flattery, a rhyming
Panegyric, I just thought a
Birthday poem would,
By its nature, contain
A more personal lyric.
…
Okay, all right … enough already!
Easy soldier. Nice and steady.
I wasn't meaning to make you mad,
But given I have, or momentarily had,
Appropriately chastened, I hasten to add …

FEAR SOME (NOT OTHERS)

The strange thing is,
you were the one
who leapt onto the
plastic chair,
shrieking, when
first we met: me,
with my whelping
bark & needle teeth,
the object of
your terror. And
then, when they
finally coaxed you
into holding me, your
hands trembled,
hovered
above my pelt, fearful
of the bristling
power between us.

Now though that
the others more or
less ignore me
because I have so
little left to give—

no cuddles, zest,
obedience—it's
those same hands
(grown, nails painted)
that tender my
blindness, calming
the night rushing
through me. Now
that balls bounce by
without my notice,
my hind legs too
withered to walk
free from pain,
it is your bed
that pillows
my bag of jutting
bone, and you,
the scared one,
who has become
my scent of home.

September 2021

DRIVING LESSONS

Lesson 1: *Check the Mirrors*
Mainly you want to look ahead,
But it's important to know
Where you've come from,
Who's behind, who's got
Your back, who's tailing
Your gate.

Lesson 2: *Blind Spots*
Here, mirrors are no help.
Not even head checks.
We all have them:
Things we cannot see. All you
Can do is know they are there:
Fears, doubts,
Phantoms on your fender.

Lesson 3: *Ease and Squeeze*
No sudden movements, nothing gross.
Everything's micro nowadays,
Incremental adjustments,
No grand gestures. All of it
Power-assisted:
Steering, the brakes.

Ease on the accelerator,
Squeeze to a stop.
By all means tickle the machine,
But don't cede to it
Your driver's seat.

Lesson 4: *In Traffic*
Try not to pressure those in front of you,
Give them room to make mistakes.
Treat everyone on the road
As fool & fellow-traveller both,
All of them, like you,
making their way through
the madness
they too help to create.

Lesson 5: *Yielding*
Sometimes it's good to let them in,
To give way, wave them on.
And then there's the ones you
Need to think for more than of,
Who believe the road
Came as part of the package
When they bought their prestige car.
Scream at them, of course (they cannot hear),
But know there will be times when
You too will err in judgement

Or from inattention, and your duco
—Even your life—will depend on the
Awareness of others.

Lesson 6: *Cornering*
Obviously straight roads
Are the safest. And most
Boring; resisting sleep their biggest
Challenge. So, sure, take
The winding one & enjoy the view,
The feel of the car mapping
Mountain or coast. But be sure
To brake when entering bends
And always accelerate as you
Leave the thrill of them behind.

Lesson 7: *Return Journey*
Now that I've taught you
What little I know—my
Abilities already eclipsed by
Your parallel parking: What next,
Backing trailers?—
Wherever you are, whatever
Your vehicle
—Bike, car or bus—
Be sure to steer it
Now and then

Down the road between
You and me
On your way
Back to us.

September 2022

THE DIARY OF AMOS BOYLE

23 November 1857

Again, I have not attended to this duty for some
weeks. Life is hard enough in the living without
me spending my nights worrying it over on the
page. I have turned every sod on my claim and have
nothing but blisters and an aching back to show for
it. This past month I have worked Maloney's battery.
For a day or so we were finding half an ounce a
day. Then Maloney took to the grog, drinking his
luck away. By the time he had dried out, so had the
seam. Then yesterday part of the shaft caved in. I was
working the battery up top. Now that the mud has
dried out, the dust on the diggings is like a London
fog; I couldn't see two feet in front of me. And the
cracking of the rocks made it hard to hear. But then,
wiping my brow, letting the cradle rest a moment,
I heard his screaming; cusses and curses that will
surely gain him entry into Hell. In my hurry to
reach him, scrambling down the embankment,
crawling into the shaft, I forgot to take a lamp. His,
it seemed, had been extinguished in the cave-in.
With the darkness pushing in around me, the dust
filling my lungs, it was all I could do not to panic. I

thought of Father and the story he always told of the
cave-in of '33, back in Cornwall. Picturing his face,
the black lines spreading out from his eyes when
he told us those stories, his voice a whisper, then a
boom, it calmed me, and I crawled on and found
Maloney half buried, still swearing. Scooping the
rocks and dirt out with my hands—Maloney helping
with his free arm, all the time abusing me—I finally
pulled him free. His left foot looked to be in a bad
way. I hauled him back above ground, just as I have
hauled him now from the Pick & Barrow. By his
snoring, I doubt his foot is paining him much now.

Today's close shave has made my mind up. I
have been thinking about it for some time, ever since
I abandoned my claim, but now I am decided—I
am leaving the Ballarat. Truth be known, it is only
stubborn pride that has kept me here this long;
Mammy's words ringing in my empty head, "It's a
big chance you're taking, risking your life, losing
your loved ones, to chase a rainbow." Well, Mammy,
my rainbow chasing days are over; I do not want
to die in a dusty mine shaft. I am striking out for
Melbourne town come morning.

28 November 1857

There is not the time to tell of all the sights I have

seen these past five days. The excitement began
not far from the diggings when a man on a horse
galloped up to the cart I was riding on, yelling and
waving his hands. I thought he was a bushranger,
one of these high-way bandits that hold up coaches.
It turned out his wife was giving birth in a camp
close by and he was hoping one of us might be
a doctor. All of us on the cart were only miners,
though the fellow next to me said he had helped
birth a calf once. Everyone laughed, and the worried
father-to-be rode off in a cloud of dust.

Melbourne is growing apace. Whole city
blocks, whole settlements, have shot up like spring
grass since last I was here. I made my own camp a
few miles up the river. Last night, lying in my tent,
I heard this far off moaning sound and something
going clack, clack, clack, like a clock keeping
time. At first I thought the sounds must have been
coming from another of the strange animals that
inhabit these parts, but after a while, once I got my
courage up, I looked out of the tent and saw the
glow and shadows of a large fire burning further
up the river bank. It was the Blacks, having some
sort of ceremony. I crept towards them, crouching
low, trying not to make a sound. The moaning
noise seemed to be made by men blowing into thin,
hollow logs and the clacking came from other men

clapping sticks together. I watched for what must have been over an hour as they danced and stamped and sang wailing hymns to their pagan gods. Some were all but naked, covered in some sort of oil and dotted with what looked like white paint, while others, perhaps the older ones, wore long fur capes to protect them from the evening chill. I do not mind confessing, I found the whole affair quite fascinating. I was scared at first, but after a while, the fear left me. They knew I was there—everyone in the colony says you cannot creep up on a black man—but they let me watch regardless.

3 December 1857

I have been too exhausted to write. Life, it seems, is either too boring or too busy to write about. Of late, it has been too much the latter. I met a man named Wallace Taylor who said he could find me some work at the Port. For four days now we have been loading bales of wool onto schooners bound for home. To think I left the diggings because the work was too hard and dangerous! A man died at the Port last week, crushed by a pile of bales that collapsed in a ship's hull. If I was not so tired, or so proud, I might have hatched a plan by now to stowaway on one of these ships. I do miss my kith and kin so. I dream most every night of Mammy's stew and her great steaming puddings. What I would give to sup at her table this very night! Ah, but that is the price of adventure. Or so I tell myself.

5 December 1857

Not a stowaway, but the next best thing! The Captain of a schooner, the Margaret Nicol, has agreed to take me on as a deckhand. He has lost half his crew to the rumour of another strike up near Forest Creek. I thought of trying my luck there, too, but I have decided to put rainbows behind me for good and to swallow my pride and return to Falmouth. We set sail first light tomorrow and should be in England before Spring!

7 December 1857

I write now as a record, in case my luck continues on this wretched course and I am dead and someone later finds this journal and so will know my fate and that of my fellow crewmen. We put to sea two days ago under fine skies. We were not five leagues beyond Port Phillip Bay, though, when the winds picked up and dark clouds covered us. The Captain was experienced and seemed well in control, but it was all hands on deck throughout the day and into the night. The rumour was he planned to drop anchor on the leeward side of an island, to take shelter for the night, to see off the storm. The schooner lurched in all directions, tossed and blown like a leaf. I was trying to retie a rope on the mainsail when I heard a tremendous crash. It was as if the Heavens themselves had rent in two. If I had not been holding the rope, I would have been thrown overboard right there and then. As it was, I flew across the deck like a harpoon, jolting to a screaming stop when I reached the end of my tether. The noise was tremendous, like a giant grinding his teeth. The Margaret Nicol, it seems, had foundered on rock; her hull being gouged to pieces. Perhaps the bales plugged the hole, but for an eerie moment everything went silent and still. Then there was another wave, another enormous cracking of wood on rock, and the ship listed portside. I let go of the rope and slid across the deck, dangling from the gunwale. The last thing I remember clearly was my fingers clinging desperately to that worn, slippery wood.

The next few hours are blank pages in the book of my memory. I imagine I hit my head on the hull as I fell into the sea. Somehow, by some miracle, I landed, or in my senseless state, clambered upon the plank of wood that saved my life. I am no great swimmer, so it was only good fortune or the mercy of God that delivered me safely to land. It was still dark when I awoke, washed up upon a beach, the plank still beneath me; my self, a piece of driftwood. Though the storm had eased, the waves were still enormous, but ebbing, leaving me to this drier Fate. My head was cleft with pain, though I could find no blood. I dragged myself into the bushes above the sand and drifted on sleep—much as I had upon the storm's savage swell—until morning light.

I have spent these past hours scouring the shore for fellow survivors, collecting what flotsam had been washed up with me from the wreckage. The Margaret Nicol is completely sunk, and I can only guess at the rocks upon which she foundered. Alas, I seem to be the sole survivor. I did, though, find one of my fellow crewmen, Arnold Bailey— dead, his torso draped in seaweed, the birds already pecking at his remains. I dug him a resting place in the sand and hauled his waterlogged body, the flesh all blue and bloated, and eased him into his shallow grave. Saying the Lord's Prayer over his mound, I succumbed to feelings of desperate loneliness, to my fear and grief, and wept on Bailey's tomb like I were his own mother.

I did find some useful items washed up on

the shoreline: 1 bottle of Sanderson's rum; 7 good
lengths of planking (along with many shorter,
broken pieces of lumber); a torn section of sail about
the size of a large blanket; 3 tins of potted meat; and
1 empty mustard jar. I must also confess to stripping
Bailey of his outer garments and of filching his good
leather belt and the knife that hung from it. The
bounty on my own person was less rewarding—1
kerchief; 1 pipe (stem broken); 1 pouch of sodden
tobacco; 1 flint; and the key to my chest. It was,
though, the discovery of this very book and pen
in the inner pocket of my waistcoat that most
gladdened my heart. I am not sure why. A form of
companionship, perhaps? Regardless, it set me on
a fool's errand, as I spent time that I should have
used to find food, burning wood to make ink from
charcoal and ground-up rock and water, which I
now have captured in my mustard jar.

8 December 1957

The days are warm, but the nights, when the wind
picks up, are cold. I have made a rough shelter
in amongst some rocks from the planks and the
branches of trees, but not it, nor the sail, nor Bailey's
clothes could keep out the freezing wind.
Today I explored further afield and made the dismal

discovery that I am tossed up upon an island. I have circumnavigated it now and have yet to find human habitation, though I found an old campfire on the western shore, close by some rock pools that offered me up a meal of mussels. The northern tip of the island is like a finger of land, pointing to the mainland, which is no more than a league or two across the sea. There is no sign of human habitation there either, though I thought I saw smoke in the far off distance. I expect there are tribes of natives living in that density of bush.

The middle of the island remains a mystery to me. Perhaps some natives live there, inland. I will explore it on the morrow. For now, I must make the most of the dwindling light and build a fire big enough to warm me through the night.

10 December 1857

I did not write yesterday from exhaustion. I traversed the island's blank interior. No sign of natives. I found a creek, more a runnel of water, and I spent today carrying my planks of wood and other precious possessions to the north western shore, where there is water and I will be more sheltered from the wind. I keep myself busy to ward off the loneliness, to keep my panic at bay. I have only 1 tin of potted meat left.

11 December 1857

I spent all day trying to catch a fish, using Bailey's
bootlaces for a line and a bent nail from a plank
as a hook. I had 3 nibbles, but the rogues all took
my bait and beat a hasty retreat. At one point my
frustration became fury as I tossed the tackle into the
sea. Realising my folly, I quickly stripped myself bare
and dove in after it. I later found more mussels and
ate them, keeping the potted meat in reserve. I am
hungry all the time. My gut feels hollowed-out, the
morsels I drop in it echoing like a pebbles dropped
in a well. I am dizzy, too. Whenever I stand, my
head goes to sea. I flit back and forth from curses
to prayers; cursing my luck, praying it will change.
I picture Mammy and baby Ella (who is no more a
baby, I guess) and I weep.

15 December 1857

I have not written for fear of giving flight to
thoughts of despair. I spent all of one day hunting
gulls with a spear fashioned from Bailey's knife.
After hours of failed attempts, I winged one and
dove upon the wretch like the desperate dog I have
become. The bird's flesh was tough and oily and sat
like a slick on the shallow waters of my stomach.

Still, I am sure it gave me strength.

That night, when the sun went down, it was as if it had set in my own fiery skin. My face and neck were badly burned, pulled tighter than a drum. I used the grease from the gull's carcass as a balm, and the next morning I was swarmed by flies. I laughed at that as I plunged into the ocean and washed away the flies, the gull grease, and scrubbed at my deeper fears.

17 December 1857

Today, the skin on my neck is coming off in strips. I have lost pounds of weight and my clothes are turning to rags. Yesterday, when I was looking for eggs among the cliffs on the eastern shore (no luck!), I saw a ship crawl across the far horizon. Of course, those on board could not see or hear me, but that did not stop me jumping up and down, waving my arms, yelling until I was hoarse. Watching that sloop dwindle from sight was a kind of death for me. But from that, my hope has been resurrected. I have decided that I must make it to the mainland. The distance is not great, and if I make a new shelter from branches and scrub, I think I can fashion some sort of raft from the Nicol's old planks. Perhaps I will drown, or I will make it to other side and find no human help, but at least it gives me a chance. Left here, I will starve, or go crazy with sorrow and despair.

20 December 1857

I think it is three days since last I wrote—I have been so busy making a new shelter and working on the raft that I have lost track. Binding the planks together is proving difficult. I have experimented with seaweed, but yesterday I found a long, tussocky grass that I think may be stronger. My hunting and fishing exploits continue to be more comical than nourishing. Two days ago, I did manage to catch a fish; though its tiny size made me think I should use it for bait to lure something more substantial. Then yesterday I spent a fruitless morning trying to trap green parrots with my newest invention, a bird net made of Bailey's trousers, the bottom of the legs tied closed. The problem was, the trousers filled with so much air that I could not propel the net fast enough to catch the birds. In the end, sitting despondently watching the birds as the taunted me, flitting from tree to tree, I observed that they were feasting on tiny red berries. So, instead of eating the parrots, I ate what the parrots were eating—berries. Unfortunately, my constitution is arranged along

different lines than that of a green parrot, and I have
been regularly squatting in the grass ever since!

Christmas Eve 1857

The raft is built. I am no shipwright, but I think it is
sea-worthy enough to make the journey. It even has
a mast, which I will have to hold in place, and the
piece of sail from the Nicol will return to its original
occupation. It is appropriate, given the date (if I have
it right), that I feel the same nervous anticipation I
used to feel as boy the night before Christmas. Of
course, I know no Christmas pudding awaits me
on that other shore, but . . . Ah, Mammy. I leave
tomorrow, a short leg of a much longer voyage,
which, in God I trust, will one day take me home.

Christmas Day 1857

I have both laughed and cried this morning. I seem
to have lost yesterday's hope and optimism. When I
awoke I was paralysed by the thought that even if I
make the crossing, my plight on the mainland might
be worse than it is here. At least here I have shelter,
fresh water, and shell fish. Then a skiffle drifted
across the coast, the raindrops barely touching the
ground, and the sun came back out and with it a

rainbow, one end of which hovered near the highest peak of the mountains on the mainland. I hooted like a madman. So, despite myself, it seems I am destined to chase rainbows, misty dreams, colours in the air.

I am taking my one remaining tin of potted meat with me (the bottle of Sanderson's rum was long ago drained), but I am leaving this journal, my most precious possession, here, as an act of faith that I will find truer companions on the other side, but also as insurance, in case I drown in the attempt. I will bury this in what's left of Bailey's shirt and hope that some day hence a visitor to this windswept rock will find it and will read this true account of the survival of me, Amos Boyle, Cornishman, son of a tin miner, chaser of rainbows.

I wish you well and my self, God's speed.

Original manuscript uncovered on Gabo Island, September 2007